FOR HER...

She said, "one day you will write me one of those beautiful poems."

So, I wrote her a book...

As beautiful as a sunset the light fragments around her
As if she were the magnet that brought it all together
Her passion is like a volcano
Churning and producing heat even while dormant
Yet when it explodes, it rains fire and magma that can scorch the earth
She only fights for what's worth fighting for
When she argues it's not out of anger but for what she believes in
What you don't see well that's what makes this woman amazing
Everything that many crave yet few will obtain
The abuse and scars that destroyed a childhood
The countless disappointments from those she held dearest
Those self-destructive tendencies keep her from seeing
Just how perfect she is.
The heart of a caring mother intertwined with that of a warrior
Whom will never taste defeat
Oh, how I wish I could hold up a mirror so she would see herself as I do
Maybe then she would know why my heart beats
For her happiness, and my being craves hers
To bask in the glory of her bright shining energy
That I might shine as bright as her shadow

The moon reflects off the water

The stars reflect off the skies

A lifetime sitting next to you

Forever lost inside your eyes

Eyes are just eyes

Lips are just lips

Hair is just hair

Hips are just hips

A smile is just a smile

Dreams are just dreams

Wants are just wants

Ideas are just schemes

A house is just a house

A push is just a shove

Nothing makes complete sense

Everything means more once you fall in love

Each soul has its own secret scent

Sending signals for whom it is meant

Many shall come and many will go

Saying it is them, but they do not know

The color of soul with all its different hues

The passion of the heart and what it pursues

Only one understands what all it will take

To mend the heart when it does break

To comfort the soul when it does cry

To lift up a spirit when it longs to die

There is just one that is truly heaven sent

Only one soul will pick up your perfect scent

I looked everywhere for you and only found myself lost

So, I began to look for myself and it led me right to you

I was always meant to find you

As the part of me that was always lost

Dwelled inside of you all along

Underneath the stars the universe is ours

To dance to sway to run and to play

Through the fields and in between the trees

Across the rivers through the raging seas

Wherever we lay and wherever we may roam

Side by side with you I know that I am home

Block by block we build all our dreams

You plus me equals the perfect team

When we rest and the work is all done

You laying in my arms we welcome the rising sun

Through it all good and bad I stand

Like a statue carved from loves granite

I stand for you, our love, and our future

Aware of the pasts that brought us here

Yet refusing to let it be our today

Until the hourglass sheds its last grain of sand

Until the clocks stop and time ceases to exist

I stand ready to defend and protect you

To support you and all of your hopes and dreams

To you I bequeath my soul, ye my heart

With all that I am and all I will ever be

I stand because before you I only knew how to kneel

Longing for your existence to impact my life

With every breath you took I too did live

So, now I kneel worshiping the ground you tread

Basking in the shadow your radiant light provides

Though I existed for centuries without you

I now live for the first time because of you

This I decree...

My life both ends and begins in your eyes

With your touch and upon your lips

For lifetimes I have been forced to love you from a far

This has been my curse while still being my greatest gift

A love like this that lasts for thousands of years can only be seen as a gift

One day I will love you from up close

Until then know this

My soul is connected forever to yours

My love only grows in anticipation

I may love you from a far, but I love you forever

Love me like the moon

All the way through the night

Until the stars stop twinkling

Until the darkness fades out of sight

Love me like the sun

All the way throughout the day

Until the skies colors all mix together

When the daylight fades away

Love me like space and time

Like how light and sound compound

Engulfing me infinitely and completely

Without limits and without bounds

As I ponder the instances of how we met

I can't pinpoint the exact moment fate interjected

Maybe I was merely lost in the moment

Intoxicated by your voice and how your words clung to your lips

How they caressed parts of my soul no one has ever reached

Maybe I was so focused on how to respond

To such a beautiful soul and spirit

Perhaps it was the excitement of how two souls collided

Like how fireworks screech into the sky before exploding into beautiful colors

I am not sure when fate gave its subtle shove

Still in that moment as the dust settled and the smoke cleared

I knew I had found something I never knew I was seeking

Forever, wrapped beautifully in the package of you

Imagine finding your one

To be loved as you give love

Someone who cares more for you then themselves

Not just a partner but the counter part of your soul

The love of each lifetime

Reconnected after so much time apart

Just imagine

Yet fate knows no boundaries

Love knows no limits

I smell her soul

That old familiar essence of home

When my words fail me, and I struggle to adequately express myself

May my kiss speak a book worth of feelings and emotions

Let your lips translate the language of love

May your soul understand Morse code

Our heartbeats send out

I write you a love letter penned with a star

Saying I will always love you

Whether you are near, or you are far

I put it in a bottle

Send it upon the sea

Waiting for your response

A kiss sent upon a breeze

I could have lived

One hundred years

Yet never felt

What I felt

In that moment

When our hearts collided

Days fade into weeks

Months fade into years

Smiles turn into frowns

Laughter turns into tears

Light fades into dark

Night fades into the day

Run fades into walking

Leaving fades into stay

Wishes fade into dreams

Will not fades into I do

Lust fades into love

As I fade into you

Lips to lips hovering

The pause
Breath to breath

Essence to essence
Gravity's Invisible pull

Closer, deeper
Lips touch

Bodies float

Then go numb
High pitched hum

As the room spins
Teeth click as mouths begin to open
Slide of the tongue

Like a wine it seeps in
The erotic, lustful, seductive taste
Body to body

No space to be found
Slowly melting into each other
You ask what's in a kiss

The devil dances in her eyes
There's deviance in her smirk
Her mind is dirty, and there's a fire in her soul
She looks sweet and innocent on the outside
Refined and put together
She talks with intelligence and walks with a poise
Don't get too close though
Not unless you are ready for the journey of your life
To be loved fully and devoured completely
To feel the power of her soul and the might of her spirit
She will encompass your mind, and feed on your soul
Engulf you completely with her being
She is leather and she is lace
She is magic and she is energy
Everything you've ever wanted and all you will ever need

She was the song.
The words never mattered because all I heard was the melody of her voice.
The sway of her symphony.
The enigmatic crash of her soul through the madness of the surrounding sounds.
The world could be exploding and all I would hear was her.

Heart to heart, and soul to soul
What once was half is now a whole
Touch to touch sparks ignite
Passion blazes and lights up the night
The match is struck and the fire burns
Desires ache and the body yearns
Hands that travel from neck to hips
As tongues entangle, lips to lips
So much more than a chemical reaction
Sensual sultry sexual satisfaction

Meet me half way between happy ever after and once upon a time
Just passed the forever rainbow up the mountain only love can climb
There at the top there's palace made for two
Behind the big red door awaits the history of me and you
Tales from the beginning of time and spoilers of futures good and bad
The times that made us happiest and the outcomes that made us sad
Lifetime after lifetime our story never ends
Chapters where we are lovers and ones just as friends
Meet me half way between what was and what's meant to be
So many things to remember but so much still yet to see

The sun was jealous of how she glowed.

So, in defiance it refused to shine. The sky saddened by such disregard began to weep.

Unbeknownst to the war above she began to dance in the rain and play in the puddles.

The night sky was jealous of how she sparkled. So, in rebellion the stars shot across the sky.

Racing to a bitter end that served no purpose.

The moon, embarrassed by this, hid her face amongst the clouds.

Oblivious to the battle of the skies she laid in the grass, making wishes on each shooting star.

My soul was jealous of how she loved.

Without measure or expectations.

In stubbornness it convinced my mind of every possible reason to refuse such kindness.

 My heart dejected by the collusion between the soul and mind sulked.

 Playing sad symphonies upon its strings.

Unfazed by the conflict of the trinity she kept caring and showing her love.

When asked why she was so clueless to her shine, sparkle, and caring.

She smiled as if she knew all along.

When asked why she loved so hard and cared so much.

She shrugged her shoulders and simply said. "I was always meant to."

I am convinced she was made of all the most beautiful words ever penned.
As every drop of ink touched paper from the most beautiful minds she began to shape.
Era after era and century after century.
Until the stars kissed her eyes, putting that twinkle in them no one could ignore.
She is breathtaking and that explains why I struggle to speak when she is near.
Gasping to say hello and longing to show her
All the poetry and paragraphs her creators wrote to make the most amazing thing.
The periods that created her dimples and the passion that created her soul.
Written perfection comes to life to show the world.
That when you bleed belief, sweat creativity, and speak manifestation everything come to fruition

How to love....

Selflessly
  Completely
    Whole heartedly

Love even when love is not returned.
    With all of your soul.
        Even when you feel it breaking.

Finding love is like.
    Finding the most fragrant rose.
        In the only crack in a concrete jungle.

From beginning until the end.
    Love knows not where or why.
        It is infinite and all encompassing.

So, until you draw your last breath.
    Love, with every heartbeat.
        With every ounce of life.
                        Love....

In an instant life as we knew it changed
We had found what we had always searched for
We found love and peace happiness and home
Wrapped comfortably in each other's arms
Lost in every part of you
Loves highway took me from your mind down to your heart
As I got familiar with the path the road got rocky
You see the easiest journeys tend to be the straightest paths
Yet when I departed your heart with the destination of your soul
We began the trek over potholes in the armor
Scars of battles lost, and wounds scabbed over still bleeding.
The scattered broken pieces of lost loves and broken promises
The forest of emotions turning from light to dark the further the wander
As I approach the fortress of your soul I finally realize
Being lost in your love is the only lost I will never recover from

Inside us burns an eternal flame fueled by our love
The world could stop turning and be ravished by destruction
Our souls would still burn bright enough to illuminate the black night
Each lifetime the flame flickers like a signal so we can see the way home
Though many may add sparks to the flame
Only we can sustain it constantly
The closer we draw the brighter it glows
As we crash together again the world spins counterclockwise
The tides change and the plates all shift.
All at the touch of a hand and the softest of kisses

How was it that wide awake I still see you like a dream
Your light so radiant from the universe dwelling within your eyes
I stand blinded yet never could see more clearly
That you are not only my best love or last love.
You are love personified.
Every known word composes you to make the most beautiful poetry
Words I willingly recite for the rest of my life.

Will you ever know what you mean to me
That there's more here than what we see
Do you understand how I care for you
I'm enchanted by everything you do
How your voice soothes my entire soul
Takes all my broken pieces and makes me whole
What once was barren now beauty revealed
Like seeds planted in gardens or fertile fields
How those nurtured feelings slowly grew
Leading to heart filled whispers of I love you
Two souls melding together and becoming one
Entangling into knots that can't be undone
I will always be thankful how our stars aligned
Taking us from lost to forever intertwined

You appeared before me at the perfect time
My words all broken now they start to rhyme
Your presence of caring your heart oh so kind
You occupy my thoughts and are always on my mind
You show me what being loved is all about
Soothing my restless heart, and erasing all my doubt
Your voice embedded in the fibers of my ears
Easing my anxious spirit and erasing all my fears
I feel your arms around me even though you are not here
Making seconds feel like hours and days feel like years
I'm not sure how I made it without as long as I did
The universe had a plan, but decided to keep it hid
Until the perfect date and time so our paths would intersect
It was that exact moment that fate did interject
Sending two shooting stars blazing across the skies
I saw them as they crash landed and how they twinkle in your eyes
Lifetimes I have searched to love never quite knowing how
In you I've found the way, and my forever is starting now

I only see you and how amazing you are
I see your love for me and mine for you
I see the happiness we bring each other
Two broken people loving the pieces back together slowly
I only see you

Time is unmeasurable and space uncontainable
Our love above all this does transcend
Therefore I shall dance with you in life and death
For I am yours until the end

Who are you were you sent from the divine
Are you late or are you just in time
Were you sent to make me strong
Maybe to show me how right it is to be wrong
You smell of euphoria and make sin taste delicious
Are you here to undo me with that smirk so vicious
Each step closer you take is a bigger tease
Especially when you whisper all good girls say please
You bite your lip before your kiss bites mine
As my fingers trace your curves and then down your spine
Who are you did my scent lead you to me
Am I the hunter or the prey eyes so blurry I can't see
On your knees looking up waiting for direction
You are in my blood stream a sensual infection

Kiss me to death
Then breathe me to life
Love me fully and completely
Give my heart wings and teach it to fly
Find me trapped in the spaces in between
Then set me free
Be my salvation and be my life

Lips locked and tongues tied
Fingers graze as hands slide
Hovering nose to chin
Deep inhale I take you in
All your passions all your dreams
In my lungs and blood stream
Silence screams where we lay
As our bodies speak what mouths can't say

47

Some stories are short and take little effort or ink
Others have chapters and form an entire book
Ours is a story that started before ink was created
Before chisel was set to stone
As darkness surrounded all things and there was only space
Made from the same stardust, moon, and particles
Two souls molded from one core would drift like the tides
To crash against the shores of life
Over and over like the waves of the ocean
Always finding its home on the sand
Each time pulling more and more of home back as its journey starts over
A never-ending story painted in the stars on the canvas of the skies

Hand in hand
Side by side
Soul to soul
Galaxies collide
Lips to lips
Sets the fire
Burn down the world
With pure desire
Bodies melt together
Brains filled with lust
Causing shooting stars
Spelling I love you in their dust

Little I love you's every day
Those words mean more than I can say
Small gifts picked up just for you
To show I think of you in all I do
Those moments with you in my arms
Safe and secure from all hurt and harm
Asking if you're okay or how was your day
Dancing in the rain like children at play
With you is my home and where I'll stay
Wherever you are I long to be there
I don't need one day a year to show I care

Kiss me with the fires of a thousand sun's
Your morphine drip it gets me high
Set my soul a blaze with just one touch
Burn me down from the inside
What a way to die

Inject me with your love tap it into my veins
Dirty up my imagination until you are all that remains
Giving me a taste of Eden while at the gates of hell
Lock me up in your prison with your body as my cell

We are taught fairy tales are just make believe

A way to show a story from beginning to end

That even in the most difficult of circumstances

Beauty and love is in everything

In the end the two main characters find each other

Completing the story and leaving us with a happy ever after

I never believed in fairy tales too much

Until one day I realized that I was living one

My once upon a time was the day I met you

Two people worlds apart yet so very close in proximity

As the story progressed, we see the trials and difficulties of life

How everything that was against us tried to keep us apart

Yet with every step we took we walked closer to one another

Then we crashed into each other as our paths crossed

As we journeyed the land everything was better because of you

No matter the tragedy or issue we made it through together

As our story closes, we see that we were always each other's happy ever after

I will always believe in you
Even when you don't believe in yourself
I will always build you up
Even as you are tearing yourself down
I will always stay
Even when you are adamant that I just go
I will always love you
Even when you can't or won't love yourself.
I will do all this and so much more, because I was always meant to
Before my eyes beheld the beauty of your mind and the depths of your soul
Our particles were one
Stardust blown from the moon and beams of light from the sun
collided.

        All whilst the universe spoke you will love each other day and night for
all eternity.

Love letters written from invisible ink

Words shouting in my ears so hard to think

Everything I ever wanted to say just to you

Lyrics written without melodies playing through

A language that only you can see and read

Every single thought mixed with every hearts plead

That one day you will find them and understand

A million feelings jotted onto paper laying in your hand

Proof that for every soul there is a perfect counterpart

The journey is long, at times we don't know where to start

Yet once you walk to paths and the signs all fall into place

Two souls become one in one perfect embrace

You are my addiction the habit I just can't break
My knees get weak with the loving that we make
Groping, touching, squeezing every single inch
Sweet sexy symmetry that make angels flinch

When we are old, and our memories start to slip

When we are aged, and we struggle to remember where our thoughts wonder

I write you a message and put it into a bottle every day

No matter how good or bad life seems to get

So, we can read a love story that is uniquely our own, and we can fall in love

 With each other more and more every day.

She will be my last first kiss

As the heavens cry with joy

That we finally have found each other

We will dance amongst the teardrops

As the rain beats a soft romantic tune

Our hearts will beat in sweet synchronization

Our pulses racing as we touch

The euphoric bliss as the veil falls to the ground

Finally, resting in the arms of forever

So, we dance in the puddles of destiny

Soaked in the showers of true love

Run head long into my arms

Crash into me

Nothing can harm you here

Safely chest to chest

Heart to heart

Let the vibrations soothe your soul

Melt into me

Becoming as one

One life, one heart, and one love

Oh, that old, fermented scent

Love mixed with tension

Passion tangled into lust

Nostalgic memories play like a reel

Flashing in the eyes like projectors

In the beginning all the way to the end

I can still taste the wine upon your lips

The smell of your hair

The curves of your hips

Ah, that old, fermented smell

I can make a million promises knowing some will never come true

Instead of broken words this oath I decree to you

When you are in your darkest hours, and you do not even want to try

I will be right there beside you wiping the tears away from your eyes

When you are at your weakest, and you are reduced to a crawl

I will be right there beside you to pick you up as you fall

I will never turn away and leave you and never cover up or lie

Even when the truth hurts, and we can't see eye to eye

I will always say I love you every single chance I get

Embedding those words inside your head so you will never ever forget

I will always try to make you laugh even when you really want to cry

When your head is pointed down, I will lift it towards the sky

I will love you for an eternity and even beyond death

I will love you with all I am with every single breath

Anyone can say these words hoping to make them true

I will prove them to you every day with everything I do

I stare at you and in a moment, I see everything

The first kiss all the way until the last

The first date all the way to the wedding

I see your heart and the way it beats for us

I see your soul and how it radiates peace

I see the passion the courses through your veins

Just then I blink and finally take a breath

Your lips softly kissing mine

Eyes closed the world spins as it always does

You breathe me in and I you

Our essence filling each other's lungs

Our bodies nullifying space

Hands trembling as we touch

As time slowly restarts and reality flashes

I see the beginning and the end in your eyes

I see the axis that my world spins

I see you

I'd get lost forever in you, if you would let me
Blissfully existing in the afterglow of your soul
Breathing in your essence and surviving on the sustenance of your love

I talk to you in clips and phrases
In poems and sonnets
Prose and rhythmic syllables
My lips confess my heart's reprise
Yet my soul speaks its own language
No mind can decipher
No ear can hear
Only your soul can translate it
Hopes and dreams
Wants and desires
Soul to soul we scribe the letters of love
Our love
Our beginning and our end
A translucent never-ending love letter

QUEEN CITY STREAMS
CUZCO
LIVE STREAM MAR 1
DONETA DAWSON
NEIGHBORHOOD THEATRE
VADIM NEKHADNY NATALIE CARR EMILY SAHE
JOHNNY FLY CO.

I feel you in my heart, and you're embedded in my soul
You took my broken heart, and in time you made it whole
You're everything I am, and in everything I do
No matter how close I get, it's never close enough to you.

This is my decree:

I will spend a lifetime mending your broken heart
I will have patience as you heal
I will love you fully and unconditionally
My heart and my soul belongs to you
When you are scared I will comfort you
When you are weak I will be your strength
When you are tired I will pick up the slack
I will come whenever you call
No matter how far I will travel
For I have waited my whole life for you
I've search both high and low to find you
Now that I've found you I will never let you go
All I have is yours mind, body, and soul
My heart and my love, all for you forevermore

You are my sunshine and my starlight
You make my heart happy when you say hey.
You'll never know dear how much I care love
Please never take your smile away

Your voice so soothing it makes me melt love
It always chases the grey clouds away
When you say I love you
My knees get weak babe
It's the best way to start every day.

You are my beginning you are my ending
When you're beside me I feel at home
Your hand in mine dear
We build our lifetime
Forever is just a cloud away

We know not the time nor place love will strike
Like a snake coiled in the tall grass
We walk by it blind and clueless
Merely pawns in the universal game
Standing stargazing as we step into love's path
Then in the blink of an eye, you feel the bite
It's poison seeping through microscopic holes
Coagulating the blood making the brain and heart not function normally
Your thoughts are consumed by the other person
Feelings rushing over like waves crashing on the beach
We are slaves shackled to the pull of love's seduction
Willingly submissive to the sweet sexy passion of just a kiss

I see you and I'm frozen dead in my place
The way you smirk or that smile on your face
You're beautiful from the inside out
I finally realize what perfection is all about
From your caring eyes to your kinder heart
Your loving spirit floored me from the start
So humble and so thankful for all that you've got
It's hard to believe someone ever blew their shot
You always amaze me with everything you do
That's why I always repeat how I feel for you
I never want you to forget what you truly mean
Your presence fills up all the spaces in between
I've always wished for someone just like you
Most shocking of all, is you feel all of this too

Shh my love it is okay
For I have loved you for a million years, and I will love you for a million more
You were my first love way before we met, and will be the last one I ever know
No matter the timeline or the place on the map
I will find you
Your heart is my compass
Your soul my north star
I am never lost and can always find my way
To you... forever more....

I can't pinpoint the exact hour, minute, or second, I fell.
It seems I was neck deep treading in loves waters
Before I even knew I had jumped into its ocean
Yet here I float on the euphoric waves that crash onto your perfect shores

My favorite thing to do
To be lost in your eyes
For I declare wholeheartedly
I am completely and totally
Infatuated, enamored, and in love with you

For you see my love I struggle in vain
For no matter how I try to deny it
My heart ye my soul belongs to you
You are the cascading colors of sunrise
The breeze in the rooftops of trees
The song the bluebird sings at day break
Your voice haunts my midnight's
Your touch lingers like the dew on the grass
I surrender to your beckoning will
For I am bound already by the chains of love
Take from me this aching.. this suffering...
With just a kiss

My downfall is those eyes
Steel traps insnaring my thoughts
Submissive, I'm a slave to whatever will you beckon
Those lips perfect, supple, and articulate
The gateway to where souls go to die
Lost forever in a divine kiss
Those arms, warm, and inviting
Stealing hearts like a thief in the night
In the wake lustful, sinful, desires
Those curves dangerous and winding
Like a mountain view twisting road
Beautiful to behold and deadly to navigate
My weakness becoming my prison
Willingly and eagerly serving my sentence

LUCKY
CITY

Her scent lingers in the air
On my skin and in my nostrils
The memories flashback
Sparks and clothes flying
Lips hovering and breaths escalating
Fingers tracing as the explore
Mouths touching as bodies mingle
A slip of the tongue
Fingers dug into hips pulling her closer
Hands reading the body like braille
Eyes closed yet the visions are vivid
Her body the road map to pleasure
Destination ecstasy the arrival unknown
She melts into me and I into her
Two becoming one
One body, one soul, and one being
Her presence still lingers...

Your eyes hold a million secrets

Scars of battles and wars fought

Your deepest fears and wildest desires

So, I fall in love with you

With your mystery and starlight

I swim in the pools of your doubts

Bathe in the fires of your passion

Until I reach the doorway of your soul

That is where I find your peace and love

So, I fall in love with you again

To touch her heart to touch her skin
Her mind, her body, the deepest sin
To know her hurt to know her pains
Her passion seeping into my veins

To give her peace to show her love
I'd give her the moon and the stars above
To laugh, to love, to play, and sing
For her to know she is my everything

When I say I fall in love with you more every day
It is because I lose hours in a day blinking
Those seconds I miss whatever you are becoming or evolving into
Those split moments I will chase my entire life to catch up
Therefore, I will fall every day
Over and over in those moments
Knowing there is always more I am missing and even more to learn
My love growing from formed tears as my eyes open and close

The devil is in her eyes
There's mischief in her smirk
Almost a sadistic chuckle
There is magik in her hands
Her passion like the flames of hell
Her words drip with poison
Every word sounding like a challenge
The ferocity of a hurricane
Her walk a forbidden dance
This woman, ahh this woman

Love can't be contained be three words or eight letters

Real and true love can never be contained

You don't need to say I love you a hundred times

As if you are trying to convince your one you mean it

Everything you do and say will exude your feelings

It will be impossible to not know that love exists

It will ooze from every pore and out of every breath

Those words will be engrained as if your soul scribed them

Out of every molecule of carbon dioxide you exhale

I don't need to say anything

With just a look I can make her smile

With just a smile I can make her blush

With just a touch I can make her glow

That is what love truly looks like

Love me louder when I am silent

My demons dancing in my head

As depression seeps through the cracks in the wall

Whisper your love when life is chaotic

Let your love bounce of the insanity

When everything reaches a fever pitch, and no day has enough time

Hold me closer when I seem the furthest away

My paths get me lost and I sometimes can't find my way home

May your arms guide me and your heart be my compass

Show me forever in a glance embedded in your smile

Infinity in the softest kiss and eternity in just a touch

You are the beginning that has no end

My happily ever after

We are atoms that were created from the aftermath of exploding stars

That my love is why your eyes sparkle so

We are beams of light coming from the heavens

All the colors mixing beautifully together

That my dear is why you are a masterpiece

You are a mixture of all things infinite and unmeasurable

Our stardust must be from the same shooting stars

That is the only explanation for how I knew you

Long before introductions and formalities

I knew I loved you and that I had always loved you

They say it is better to have loved and lost

They don't know about her

How she make ideas cultivate

How she makes all my feelings stir

The way her laugh can cure all of my pains

Her spirit can wipe away all my stains

Her arms make me feel like everything is right

She can invoke safety when she holds me tight

They say to love and lost is better than not at all

As if that pain of losing is better than taking the fall

They don't know about us two

How we love without losing as others tend to do

Just like the day begins fresh and new

So does my love and feelings for you

Your souls glow shows me everything in shadows

I don't need to see things that fade

I see things that have been there for lifetimes

BULL CITY RECORDS
BULL CITY RECORDS
BULL CITY RECORDS
BULL CITY RECORDS
NEW ARRIVALS

I'll love you until my very last breath

Then I will begin the journey to find you again

For I have loved you for eternities and lifetimes

I will always find you

I will always love you

No matter what

I miss you when you are too far away

That's why I hold you tight and ask you to stay

I close my eyes, and you are all I see

I know that where you are is where I long to be

I can feel you pressed against me holding me tight

It drives my worries and fears clear out of sight

The way you love me sets my soul on fire

Your touch and kiss fill my heart with desire

Your perfect imperfections and everything you do

Makes me say every day that I want to forever keep you

True love never dies or says goodbye

It only says to be continued

Come, she beckons knowing I would follow her

To the clouds of the heavens

To the depths of hell

Just to be where she is

Like the fog dances on the lake, so does she frolic through my brain.

Filling the darkest corners with her light. Restoring my happiness and love daily.

For just the mere thought of her fills my heart with joy.

I am Icarus you are my sun.
Bright shining and glowing in my universe.
Pushing my clouds away and giving warmth in all my days.
Your attraction is so that I need to fly closer.
The warmth of your soul it beckons me.
Arrogantly I fly closer on wings of wax.
I feel them singe the closer I get.
Falling, spinning, tumbling towards the water.
I am Icarus you are my sea.
All encompassing, vast, and welcoming.
Your eyes like an ocean, glimmering yet deep
Your arms like waves rising and crashing around me.
I free fall into you, plunging into your essence.
Slowly I drown, sinking deeper and deeper.
Arrogantly I accept my situation, yea my fate.
Whether burning in your fire or drowning in your sea.
I embrace my perfect death. I crash into you.

It is not the kiss it is the closeness.

The tingling of every nerve with a touch.

The heart beating faster in anticipation.

Breathing each other in with ever inhale.

It is every nano second that is in between heaven and ecstasy.

She is as deep as the forest

Harder to leave then the brambles

Her essence is the fog at sun rise

Her beauty that of a rose

She is as guaranteed as the seasons

A memory that never will fade

A love that is ever lasting

She is forever

She is her

By the flavor of your taste

By the pressure of your lips on mine

I die a million blissful deaths

Only to be resurrected by the essence of your breath

VIRGINIA BEACH
FISHING PIER
PIER
GIFT SHOP
T-SHIRTS

I can never unlove you for you are engrained in my brain
Becoming the thoughts of midnight, and the dreams of early morning just before the alarm
I can never unlove you because you are entangled in my soul
Becoming a part of its very existence
You are a helix in its DNA making sure every lifetime you are a part of its rebirth
I can never unlove you because once you love truly it is forever
No matter the distance traveled or time past love will always exist.
It starts at the beginning of existence and is for eternity
I can never unlove you

I feel your lips upon me long after you leave
Lost in the illusions your magic seems to weave
Leaving my mind racing am I present or insane
The way you move that body forever burned inside my brain

You gave me a home

Not a building or your arms

You gave me a place I could finally fit in

A place I no longer had to act

Act as if the world was all okay

I could be broken, messy, and not all together

You allowed me to just be me

You never tried to fix me

You sat in the dark beside me

You danced with me in the sunlight

I could search the world over

Yet never find another place

A place like what I know as home

I wanted to write a song, but the words just wouldn't flow
I decided to take a drive, but I had nowhere to go
I see you in the clouds, and I hear you in the wind
I think about you all the time, and it always brings a grin

Come let go chase the stars
Palm to palm fingers intertwined
Racing reality to our hiding spot
Lay with me as our bodies melt together
On a bed of stardust under a perfect moon
Cosmic super sultry symmetry
Two hearts making loves rhythmic melody
A perfect existence until the end of time

When she kissed me, the world spun backwards

Every emotion crashed like a wave on the shore

I didn't know what life was really like

Yet I knew what forever tasted like

She walks in beauty, like the night

Of cloudless climes and starry skies

All that's best of dark and bright

Meet in her aspect and her eyes

Thus, mellowed to that tender light

Which heaven to gaudy day denies

She controlled the whole universe with her fingertips

So, why not too my whole heart

To say I fell in love with you indicates past tense.

As to say in the darkest of nights my foot striking a rock caused me to trip.

As I tumbled there you stood.

Arms open as if you too had stumbled yet had to catch yourself.

Fearing I would face the same fate you waited patiently.

When you heard my broken steps

You made every effort to make sure I would not feel the aches of falling.

 As I crashed into your arms and we both hit the ground you landed on top of me.

As I looked deeply into your eyes, I knew that I had not fallen.

I in fact was falling, and there will never be a time I am not falling.

Leaving no room for me to land.

Therefore, never needing to mutter the words I fell.

I was a spark you made me a fire
I was a ripple you made me a wave
I was I twinkle you made me a beacon
I was a word you made me a sentence
In all things I started as a beginning
Yet next to you I became my meaning

Come into me and rest for the world has left you less than
Hollowed out by destruction and empty from broken promises
Though we know not what lays ahead and only what was left behind
Rest in my arms and melt into me
Let the shackles of what scares you drop
That you may for a moment be free
Our spirits created from the same core fit perfectly into each other
So, when yours breaks down and you feel you can't go on
Rest your soul in my habitation
Let our souls once separated merge back together to form one
Making your pain my pain, and mine yours
An infinite love derived from the infinite universe
Dwelling only for a moment inside that which could never contain it
Until we explode leaving our souls to dwell forever within the cosmos

Acknowledgements:

I acknowledge that my life has been a journey

One in which I have cursed my footsteps regularly

I have many accomplishments through the years

One of my most notable though is meeting you

That fateful day when all the stars aligned

I crashed into something I was never prepared for

Many stories have been written with so many left unpenned

Ours however will always be my favorite